Copyright © 2019
All rights reserved. No part of this book may be reproduced or transmitted or stored in any form or by any means, electronic or mechanical, including photocopying, recording, or any information storage and retrieval, without permission in writing from the owner.

Urban Dictionary

will to win

The ability to do whatever is necessary in life to achieve your goals in life, sports, or any endeavor you <u>undertake</u>. <u>The will</u> to win is a phrase held by only those who truly believe in <u>the will</u> to do something that others believe one cannot do.

The Will to Win, the desire to succeed, the urge to reach your full potential… these are the keys that will unlock the door to personal excellence. – **Confucius**

The Will to Win
Competition pushes us to our best. Pursuing a goal with great intensity can certainly pay off, but it sometimes leads to more pain than gain. How much would you sacrifice for the sake of a win?
-Psychology Today

Contents

It's Possible 4

You Are The Bomb 7

Give Thanks 9

Learning From Other People Mistakes 10

Logic vs Emotions 12

Who & What I Represent 13

Will Power 14

Why Me 15

When God Says No 18

What Don't Kill You 20

The Gift & The Curse 22

It's Possible

The Will To Win

It's possible to achieve your dreams, to gain that financial freedom you always wanted. I believe everyone listening want to be successful right? But in order to be successful to live that desired lifestyle you have to have a plan in place. Goals are important to have. In fact everyone should have goals and a plan on how to reach your goals. There are so many benefits that come along with reaching your goals like.

    1). Living that desired lifestyle you always wanted to live

    2). Providing help to love ones or people in need

    3). Free-time to spend your days doing whatever it is you enjoy doing

And that's just to name a few. We need financial knowledge so that we can stop making poor financial choices due to emotions. Fear & Greed are the two most common issues we deal with and they have a large foot print on our bad decision making. Also taking advice from the wrong people. Most advice usually comes from family members, friends, or sales people. And of course our Environment, Role Models, Education, and Generational Influences all play a major part in framing our mind set. I use to own a car lot, and one of the biggest reason for closing it down was do to bad financial planning and advice from the wrong people. I should have seek advice from someone knowledgeable in the industry, but I didn't. And it put a strain on everything . See first I went to my bank and tried to get loan since I had an awesome credit history and a great credit score, but was turned around since the business wasn't even a year old. So I took out an Unconventional Loan. With the promise to pay back $3,000 a week. I knew then it sounds crazy like really what was I thinking. But because I had enough money save up at the time I thought I could handle it. And business was going great. I couldn't keep cars on the lot over 3 days. But as soon as the car sales started to slow down. I started to witness my emergency funds getting lower and lower forcing me to close down. It felt like had crashed into a building. I was in a financial disaster. See the path to reaching your goals is not always going to be a smooth ride. You will make mistakes along the way. But That's why you need to have a plan in place to help you stay the course. So always enquire, and seek advice from someone knowledgeable of that industry you in are thinking about going in. Don't give up, don't quit, and never stop believing in your dreams. Always be working on your skills remember steal sharpen steal. And do what ever required to reach your dreams so that you can enjoy all the benefits your dreams have to offer you.

You Are The Bomb

Everybody wanna be the bomb but don't know body wanna blow up! So tuck your tail in and stay on the porch... I said if you're afraid of what's rightfully yours, tuck your tail in and stay on the porch. Because this world will eat you up. This world it strives off fear, but you will never fail because you will never try. But if you never try then you will never succeed ... So lets be honest. Are you where you want to be at in life? Have you achieved all the goals you ever wanted to accomplish? So what's holding you back from going after your dreams? What's your excuse?

See fear is a silent killer, it causes stress, heart attacks ,high blood pressure, strokes. I can go on and on. So stop doubting yourself! I don't care how dark it maybe are how hard it may seem, you can get through it. Remember there's always someone else going through something tougher than you. So don't give up! K+A=S, that's KNOWLEDGE + ACTION = SUCCESS!

Give Thanks

God our father, God our father we thank you, we thank you. For the many blessing, for the many blessing. au man au man. thank you God!

Learning From Other People Mistakes

Remember learning you craft takes commitment and dedication, and you just have to find the right fit. It's so many ways to gain the knowledge that you seek, so get information on the subject that you're interested in through reading books, listening to self motivational clips, music, media shows are other entertainments even going to seminars. Push boundaries and try new ways, you just have to focus and challenge yourself daily. So pay close attention, no pain no gain. See we don't have to keep repeating the mistakes of the past and all the major set backs that comes along with it. Learn from other people mistakes so that life yields new possibilities and glorious opportunities. When I was around the age of 10 or 12 yrs old, me and 3 of my friend, we decided to hope on our bikes and ride to this creek about 10 miles up the road. Once we reached the creek, we hopped off our bikes and walked over to the bridge glancing down at the sand of the soft mud that surrounded the creek. This bridged stood about 15ft high, as we started walking towards the trail on the side of the big to the creek. Mario suggested that we jump off the bridge, we all looked around at each other and agreed. The first person to jump was Myron… He jumped off the bridge and landed on his feet with no problems, only his fingers touched the ground. As he stood back up straight he looked up at us standing on top of the bridge looking down at him… and he yelled "come on! who's next?" Terrance Sanders glanced down below closed his eyes and jumped. Landed flat on his face. As he slowly got back up dusting himself off, Mario quickly jumped! Soon as his feet hit the ground his chin hit his knees cutting the inside of his mouth. As he stood back up spitting blood out of his mouth, they all looked back up at me yelling "jump, it's your turn" I did what in person in there right mind would do. I walked down that trail on side of that bridge to the bottom of the creek.

Logic vs Emotions

Have you ever heard the saying? Leave your feelings at the door. Does logic really trump emotions? Are does emotions trump logic? Lets say you're about to make more money than you could ever make in 10 lifetimes... You're seated at the round table with 3 investors about to close the deal, when all of a sudden one of the investors blurt out something very disrespectful to you. At that very moment a since of uncertainty develops. So now your whole mood changes, what was once a professional respectful business meeting got you in your feelings. And can possible take a u turn. What do you do? Cause right now your blood is boiling and you 38 hot. But on the other hand, after you close this deal you can say whatever, however you like to this investor. What will it be? Logic or Emotions?

Who & What I Represent

Trust me I know the road to success is not always gonna be easy, so I have to remind myself daily, who I represent, what I represent. I represent God, strength, integrity, honesty, persistence, resilience, faith, my son, my family and friends. There kids my Pest Control company I can go on and on…. People admire you when you want stop. They seen you fall, they also saw when you got back up. What I'm trying is, even doe this society place so much power in money, money doesn't make you. You make the money! See if you go broke to day if you loose all your money today, you can eventually get it back. But not life, there's never gonna be another you. Don't be money whooped, whoop that money. Make that money work for you.

Will Power

As a child growing up I was always told that respect will take you a long way. That God placed his will inside of you. "Will? What is will?" Will is determination, persistence, insistence it expresses capability or sufficiency, desires, choices or even consent. It represents the future and the presence. "So what about Power?" Power? Power is the ability to act or produce an effect. To influence authority. It could be physical might or even mental. "So What if we add will and power together?" Wow! If we were to add will and power together, we would get something unstoppable. Imagine the choices you made, led you down the path to success. That by being determine and persistent, life yield to your ever desire… "Remember you reap what you sow, you can only take out what you put in."

Why Me

Have you ever asked the question, Why me? Cause see life has a funny way of sneaking up on us if you know what I mean. Unwanted situation popping up at the wrong time, and if we're not careful it can catch us off guard. having you feeling like someone just pushed up off a cliff or something. Are like having a bad dream that you can't wake up from. It could be a bad relationship gone south or a bad business deal, behind on you bills or even family issues. The list can go on and on. But the million question is… How do you deal with it? How do you handle that type of situation? But first lets touch back on the first question. Why Me? It's crazy because Less Brown response to this question was. Why not you? Who would you like to recommend?
Who did you have in mind? Do you have any suggestions? Which left me thinking like… Wow! See remember God will never place a

burden on us that we can't handle, we just have to come down and focus. So that we can gather up enough information and see it more clearly. Everything in life has a process and we just can not rush the process. Even doe we wish we could. Have you ever heard the words instant gratification? That's what we want right? We want it now and later like the candy. So now, how do we deal with it? Do we act off of our emotions and impulse? Are do we really put some thought into? Because the choices that we make to day will play a major part in our future. And remember there's always a chain reaction, we reap what we sow. So lets say you don't take the proper steps, and rush the process. What's the worst thing that can happen? How do you think it will make you feel? It's always best to have some type of insight on whatever it is you're trying to accomplish. Goals are considered to be our end point our destination. But in order to reach our goals we have to create a plan a strategy which I personally consider to be my gps. So, you have to pay close attention to our plans, making sure that we stay on course or get back on course.

So that when it's all said and done we are able to enjoy the fruits of our labor. So again… Why you? I think you already know the answer to that question. Keep moving forward because great things always come to does that hustle.

When God Says No

When God says no! I'm talking about redirection. I'm talking about a re-direction, a shift in your life. What if you worked your whole life I'm talking bout all your life you wanted to be an entertainer, a pro athlete, a doctor, a lawyer, nurse etc… but things didn't fall the way you felt they should. You did everything you could possibly do, but things still didn't workout didn't go right. See in life there's always a lesson to be learned, a reason for why things happen. See what's amazing about life is that the road you choose to take doesn't always lead you directly to your destination. You might have to turn on to travel st, then on to success lane and a whole bunch of other streets before you reach your destination. And right before you get to turn on to that st that you're suppose to be on to get to where you going. You see a big sign that says "ROAD CLOSED!!!" At this very point you can either take another route to get to your destination or you can say forget it, it's not worth it. What do you do?

What Don't Kill You

What don't kill me can only make you stronger right? I did everything I could think of, to better myself while incarcerated. I even taught a forex class. Forex is the market in which currency is traded, this is the largest most liquids market in the world and I learned it well enough to teach guys that had there own mutual fund companies. Who were in prison for inside trading, which led me to realize that I could accomplish anything that I set my mind to. No matter how big the task was, or how long it would take me. If I had to fall a million times, I would get back up again. Plus I couldn't keep repeating the past and continuing to walk down the path that led me to prison in the first place. That wasn't smart, Einstein once said that to repeat the same actions over and over again expecting a different result is insanity. I was born in a maze but now I could see clearly. I was my own worst enemy, and like the game of chest if I can't figure out my next move I'm doomed. You have to understand, they can trap your body but they can't trap your mind. That's the most powerful tool you can ever use. So you have to use it to your advantage. Like they say, "work your magic…" You can't be afraid to fail, especially us men and women that were already risking our live in the streets daily. And the only thing promised to us then, with that type of lifestyle was death or prison. With the exception of a few, but it's not that many. Our kids, family and friends all need us in there lives. We are the bread winners, so lets find a better way to provide that food on the table. Real Estate, Party Promotions, Food Trucks, Lawn Service, Car Washes etc… You know what you have to do, you just have to put your mind to it and do it. You are great beyond measure. So wake up sleeping giant, it time to go to work!

The Gift & The Curse

I was born May 19th 1978 to Marie Johnson and Kenny Clark. Growing up I truly admired my biological dad. Even doe he was really never around. I only saw him a few times that I can remember. I could probably count them on my finger. I thought he was Super man, the black clark Kent even doe his name was Kent clark. but as I grew up I started to realize that he was never around. My mom had fallen in love with a gentleman by the name of Tony Smith which later adopted me! So I understand the effects of not haven a biological father in your life. It can have you felling a little out of place, kinda left out. But I watched and saw how my stepfather treated me, It was no different from how he treated his real kids.

As I grew up he became the only the dad I knew.. He was my role model. By the time I turned 14, I was sneaking out the house, hanging on the corner, lying to my mom. Drugs had really hit our community hard and it was trickling down to the youth. So I started looking up to the drug dealers. These guys could dress and their swagger was complimented by their nice cars, large amounts of money, and women fighting over them. They seemed to have it all together. It was crazy! This lifestyle was intoxicating, it gave me a rush. See I'm a product of my environment so don't condemn me. I will never condone selling drugs even doe I did. So with what I'm about to share with you. I hope that you eat the meat and throw away the bones. Because if you say that you love me. You have to love all of me. The Good The Bad & The Ugly!

At age 17 I was kicked out of High school for fighting. I wasn't in my right mind. Because later the evening me and my crew went over to the guys I got to fighting with side of town and shot up. I was young and reckless! A very scary place to be. I was heading down the point of no return.

It only got worse, those guys I was fighting with retaliate the feud went on for at least a year. Then came the charges! All that shooting and fight and nobody was killed Thank GOD... Assault And Battery With Intent To Kill, but also my mom's cancer had spread it was getting worse. . And then came the day I wish wold have never come. May 20th 1996 a day after my birthday my mom past away. I had just turned 18 and my sister was only 8 at the time. I was really confused, didn't know which way to go. I was facing jail time and the death of my mom had me devastated. Only GOD knows what was running through my mind. Lucky me, I was only given Probation changing my charge to accessory after the fact. And the school allowed me to come back. A year and thee days after my moms death 2 of my closes friends died in a car reck. WHAT WAS GOD TELLING ME? I wanted to change but didn't know where to start. I could rap but South Carolina wasn't known for making it in the rap industry. Although there's truly a lot of great talent here, we was always over looked. Still hanging in the streets.

Now I'm at the age of 20. One night while out at the club with a couple of my friends I got into an altercation and was shot in the leg while tussling over a gun. Again, Luckily nobody was killed.

The life I was living was consuming me with pain and trouble. The kind of life many people never return from. Then in Feb of 2006 at age 26 I was federally indicted with the intent to distribute 5 kilos of cocaine and sentenced to 5yrs at Coleman Federal Prison. I can honestly say that this street life was destroying me slowly but surely it's not all that it's cracked up to be.

There's not a lot of happy endings. I will never consider myself to be a drug dealer. I'M A HUSTLER! Now that I've had an opportunity to look back over my life. I can truly say that I'm BLESSED! I COULD HAVE BEEN ANYWHERE IN THE WORLD EVEN 6 FT DEEP, BUT I'M HERE WITH YOU. I HAVE NOT NOR WILL I EVER CONSIDER MYSELF A DRUG DEALER. I'M A HUSTLER! LISTEN

I CAN SALE STOCKS ON WALL STREET OR EVEN CD'S OUT THE TRUNK OF A CAR IF MY HEART SO DESIRE IT. NEVER LIMIT YOURSELF TRUST IN GOD WITH ALL YOUR HEART IN WHATEVER YOU DO!

Made in the USA
Coppell, TX
03 February 2023